W9-CEV-933

holiday *Pumpkins*

holiday *Pumpkins*

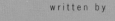

written by

GEORGEANNE BRENNAN

conceived & produced by

JENNIFER BARRY DESIGN

photography by

PENINA

Ten Speed Press

BERKELEY · TORONTO

Copyright © 1998, 2003 Jennifer Barry Design
Text copyright © 1998 Georgeanne Brennan
Photographs copyright © 1998 Penina

All rights reserved. No part of this book may be reproduced in any form,
except brief excerpts for the purpose of review, without written permission of the publisher.

A Kirsty Melville Book

Ten Speed Press
P.O. Box 7123
Berkeley, California 94707
www.tenspeed.com

Distributed in Australia by Simon & Schuster Australia, in Canada by Ten Speed Press Canada,
in New Zealand by Southern Publishers Group, in South Africa by Real Books,
and in the United Kingdom and Europe by Airlift Book Company.

Conceived and Produced by Jennifer Barry Design, Fairfax, California
Design Assistant: Leslie Barry
Layout Production: Kristen Wurz
Copy Editor: Carolyn Miller
Food Stylist: Pouké
Prop Stylist: Carol Hacker/Tableprop, San Francisco
Floral Stylist: Sarah Dawson
Craft Styling: Jennifer Martin, San Francisco
Photography Assistant: Martin Dunham
Proofreading: Barbara King

Additional photography credits:
Photograph of Pumpkin Pie on cover copyright © Joyce Oudkerk-Pool
Photographs on pages 8, 13, 21 copyright © Deborah Jones
Photograph on page 95 copyright © Jennifer Barry Design

Library of Congress Cataloging-in-Publication Data
Brennan, Georgeanne, 1943–
Holiday pumpkins : a collection of recipes, gifts, and decorations /
written by Georgeanne Brennan, Jennifer Barry ; photography by Penina.
     p.   cm.
"A Kirsty Melville Book."
ISBN 1-58008-535-0 (pbk.)
1. Cookery (Pumpkin)   2. Pumpkin.   I. Barry, Jennifer.   II. Title.
     TX803.P93 B7423   2003
     641.6'562—dc21   2003003861

First printing, 2003
Printed in Hong Kong

10 9 8 7 6 5 4 3 2 1 — 07 06 05 04 03

R03062 01097

Acknowledgments

Georgeanne Brennan would like to thank the following people:
My husband, Jim Schrupp, for his enthusiastic recipe testing and astute editing.
My children, Ethel, Oliver, Tom, and Dan, and their friends, all of whom
sampled and critiqued numerous pumpkin recipes. Jennifer Barry for asking me
to participate in this project and for allowing me to be part of one
of her many beautiful books. Charlotte Kimball, Tom Neely, and Tom Olson for their
thoughtful recipe testing and opinions. Carolyn Miller for her diligent editing.

Jennifer Barry Design and the photography and styling team would like
to thank and acknowledge the following individuals for their help on this book project:
Marta Hallett and editor Gabrielle Pecarsky for their enthusiastic support
and guidance; Melissa Hacker for prop styling assistance; for props: El Plato and
Barbara Chambers/Spenser House, San Francisco; Marilyn Martin for craft styling assistance;
assistance with flowers and produce: David Bache at Brannan Street, Nozaki Enterprises,
Green Valley Growers, Tierra Vegetables, and Phillips Farms from the Marin County
Farmers Market; Kristen and Everett Wurz for Halloween modeling assistance;
Tom Johnson for production assistance; and Maria Hjelm for marketing support.

1

introduction

9

Choosing a Pumpkin for Cooking

How to Cook a Pumpkin

Baking Whole Pumpkins

Baking Pumpkin Halves
or Wedges

Steaming Pumpkin Wedges,
Slices, or Cubes

Preparing Raw Pumpkin
Wedges or Cubes

Cooking with
Pumpkin Blossoms

2

soups, stews, & salads

recipes 15

Pumpkin-Ginger Soup Topped
with Crème Fraîche and Condiments

Pumpkin and Black Bean Soup

Pumpkin Soup Topped
with Croutons and Fresh Thyme

Beef and Pumpkin Stew
with Pomegranates

Roasted Pumpkin Seeds

Spinach and Pumpkin Seed Salad

Frisée Salad with
Deep-Fried Pumpkin Bits and Lardons

Butterhead Lettuce and Pumpkin
Blossom Salad

Root Vegetable and Pumpkin Ragout

3

tabletop pumpkins

crafts 31

Pumpkin Place Cards

Pumpkin Candle Holders

Pumpkin Soup Tureen
with Mini-Pumpkin Condiment Bowls

Three Pumpkin Centerpieces

Pumpkin Vase

4

grills & savories

recipes 45

Honey-Grilled Pumpkin Slices

Sautéed Pumpkin, Red Peppers,
and Greens with Polenta

Pumpkin Blossoms
with Goat Cheese Filling

Pumpkin Pasta with Baby Bok Choy,
Prosciutto, and Pecans

Scalloped Pumpkin and Potatoes

Pumpkins and Mixed Winter Squash
Filled with Savory Puree

Pumpkin and Chanterelle
Mushroom Risotto

Whipped Pumpkin on Caramelized
Onions with Spicy Walnuts

Baked Pumpkins Stuffed
with Sausage and Sage

Grilled Quail with
Herbed Mashed Pumpkin

pumpkin desserts

breads,
muffins, & cookies

outdoor pumpkins

pumpkins for kids

recipes 77

Pumpkin Cheesecake in a
Gingersnap-Walnut Crust

Pumpkin-Filled Phyllo Cups

Pumpkin Flan

Harvest Pie

Old-Fashioned Pumpkin Pie

Pumpkin Ice Cream

recipes 97

Pumpkin and Pecan Pancakes

Halloween Cookies

Pumpkin Bars with Lemon Glaze

Pumpkin and Medjool Date Muffins

Pumpkin Bread

Metric Conversions

List of Recipes

List of Crafts

Index

crafts 63

Pumpkin Wreath

Pumpkin Harvest Swag

Hanging Mini Monsters

Parchment- or Tissue-Lined
Jack-O'-Lanterns

Woodcarving Jack-O'-Lanterns

crafts 89

Painted and Appliquéd Pumpkins

Papier-Mâché Trick-or-Treat Baskets

Halloween Cookie Tree

Introduction

Pumpkins are woven into our history, myth, and lore. The hard-skinned fruits are as much a part of our cuisine as they are symbols of autumn and winter in our culture. Pumpkin pies, cookies, breads, and ice cream speak of the season, along with pumpkin soups and stews, pumpkin puree with herbs and butter or honey and ginger, and toasted pumpkin seeds. Pilgrims, pumpkins, and the first Thanksgiving in the New World are synonymous. Each year we renew our thanks and celebrate the season of plenty with feasting tables decked with pumpkins, apples, and grapes.

In American literature, the headless horseman of Washington Irving's tale terrifies the schoolmaster Ichabod Crane by hurling a head, revealed later to be a pumpkin, at the hapless master. Jack Pumpkinhead is one of the most beloved characters in Frank L. Baum's classic stories from the Land of Oz; with his sensible pumpkinhead stuck firmly on the wooden stake between his shoulders, his exploits are the marvel of the country-side. Although European in origin, the tale of Cinderella and her magical pumpkin coach has been adopted by American children for generations.

But nowhere is the lore of the pumpkin more evident than in the jack-o'-lanterns of Halloween, when eerie faces carved into pumpkins are candlelit from within, then set out to keep away the ghosts that, according to legend, return each October 31 on All Hallows' Eve. This tradition came to North America with the Irish, who immigrated to the eastern seaboard. In Irish folklore, Jack—who made a deal with the devil and then tricked him—was denied entrance to both heaven and hell, but when the devil cast him into eternal darkness he gave him an ember to light his way. In Ireland, All Hallows' Eve was celebrated by carrying an ember in a hollowed-out turnip, but in America, pumpkins replaced turnips.

Pumpkins originated in the New World, where they have been cultivated for several thousand years. Hard-skinned winter squashes, pumpkins are eaten when fully mature. Round, oval, or even elongated, they have orange flesh, while their skin color can range from orange to white, buff, red, and even bluish green.

Winter squash originated in southern Mexico and spread throughout the Americas. Pumpkins, long a staple of Native American food by the time the Pilgrims arrived, soon became a staple for the Pilgrims as well, for pumpkins were easy to grow, stored well, and provided nourishment throughout the winter.

Pumpkins have a mild flesh that lends itself to both sweet and savory treatments. In soups and stews, it takes on the flavor of broth and herbs, while in pies, cakes, and breads, it contributes moisture, lightness, and color and marries well with spices such as cinnamon, ginger, mace, and nutmeg. In savory dishes, sautéed or baked pumpkin is a ready companion to complementary ingredients such as cheese, butter, herbs, rice, and pasta.

Choosing a Pumpkin for Cooking

While all pumpkins can be used for cooking, the best ones are those with a relatively small seed cavity and thick, flavorful flesh that is fine-grained rather than fibrous. The round Sugar Pie (also known as New England Pie, Small Sugar, Boston Pie, and Northeast Pie) is one of the most common and flavorful of cooking pumpkins. Although they generally range in size from 6 to 8 pounds, smaller ones weighing 2 to 4 pounds can often be found. "Cheese" or "cheese-box" pumpkins, which are round,

squat, and flattened like a cheese wheel or tall like a cheese box, are also thick-fleshed with a sweet flavor and a fine texture. Some of the commonly found varieties are Cheese, Big Cheese, and Long Cheese.

Their skin might be white, orange, beige, or even red, such as the French heirloom variety, Rouge Vif d'Etampes, sometimes called the Cinderella pumpkin because its flattened, deeply lobed shape resembles early illustrations of Cinderella's coach. The white or orange mini pumpkins that have become so popular, such as Jack-Be-Little, are also excellent for eating, though because of their small size they don't have much flesh. In France, a good cooking pumpkin is the deeply lobed, buff-colored Musqué de Provence or Muscade. It has a very small seed cavity and thick walls of bright orange, fine-textured flesh. These large pumpkins, usually 20 to 35 pounds, are sold by the wedge rather than whole.

Some of the very largest pumpkins, such as Big Max, are considered good eating, but their size makes them impractical for most home cooks.

A cooking pumpkin should feel heavy in the hand, indicating a good flesh-to-cavity ratio, and be firm, not soft, to the touch. The stem should be attached to maintain the protective integrity of the skin.

Pumpkins will store for months if kept in a cool, dry place. Once cut, they will keep a few days in the refrigerator, wrapped in plastic wrap.

How to Cook a Pumpkin

Pumpkin is usually precooked before being used in a dish. This can be accomplished in a number of different ways, depending upon the desired end use. Pumpkin puree, commonly used in pumpkin recipes and to make pumpkin pie, is made by first baking a pumpkin, either whole or in halves or wedges, then pureeing the pumpkin flesh. Remember, the texture of the puree will depend on the type of pumpkin you use, with cooking pumpkins yielding the finer puree, the carving and ornamental the more fibrous. Store pumpkin puree in an airtight container in the refrigerator for up to 4 days.

Baking Whole Pumpkins

When a recipe calls for soft or pureed pumpkin, it is easiest to simply bake a whole pumpkin. Once cooked, it is easily peeled, seeded, and mashed.

Place a whole pumpkin weighing about 3 or 4 pounds on a baking sheet and bake at 350°F until a sharp knife easily pierces through to the seed cavity, about 1-1/2 hours. Smaller pumpkins will require less time. Remove the pumpkin and let it cool. When it is cool enough to handle, peel the skin away with a knife. Cut the pumpkin in half, scoop out the seeds and their fibers with a large spoon and discard them. Finally, mash the flesh by hand with a potato masher, or process it in a food processor. The pureed flesh is now ready to use in recipes calling for pumpkin puree.

If you don't have time to make your own, especially if you need only a small amount, canned pumpkin puree is a good substitute.

Baking Pumpkin Halves or Wedges

Most pumpkins over 6 or 7 pounds are too large to fit in a standard oven, but they can be baked in halves or wedges. To cut the pumpkin in half, push the tip of a large, stiff knife into the seed cavity at the top of the pumpkin, next to the stem, then cut down the side to the base. Repeat on the other side. Scoop out the seeds and fibers with a spoon and discard them. To bake the pumpkin for puree, leave it in halves. To make single servings of baked pumpkin, cut the halves into wedges.

To bake pumpkin for puree, place halves, cut side down, on a baking sheet and bake at 350°F until the flesh is easily pierced with a knife, 40 minutes to an hour. To bake wedges for single servings, season them with butter and salt and pepper, or butter and brown sugar, and bake them, cut side up, at 350 °F until tender, about 15 to 20 minutes.

Remove and let cool. To make a puree, scoop out the flesh and discard the skin. Mash with a potato masher or process in a food processor.

Steaming Pumpkin Wedges, Slices, or Cubes

Cut the unpeeled pumpkin into the desired size and scoop out the seeds and fibers. Place the pieces in a steaming basket and steam over boiling water in a large pot. Cover and steam until tender when pierced with a knife, about 15 minutes. Remove from the steamer and let cool, then peel and use. Alternatively, cubes can be cut from wedges after steaming.

Preparing Raw Pumpkin Wedges or Cubes

To use uncooked pumpkin, usually in savory dishes, the pumpkin must be peeled first. Cut the pumpkin in half, scooping out and discarding the seeds and fibers. Using a sharp knife, peel the pumpkin halves, and then cut the pumpkin into wedges or cubes of the desired size.

Cooking with Pumpkin Blossoms

Pumpkin or other squash blossoms are either male or female. The female blossoms have a small, distinct pumpkin at the base. The male blossoms, however, simply have a stem. Either male or female blossoms may be used for cooking. Whether the blossoms are from your garden or purchased, inspect them inside before using them, as they are often home to pollinating insects. If the blossoms are closed, reopen them by submerging them in their entirety in ice water for a minute or two. The golden yellow, slightly furry stamen can be bitter, so you may wish to remove it before stuffing or otherwise using the blossoms.

Pumpkin or squash blossoms may be stored in the refrigerator in a sealed plastic bag, and the stems of the male blossoms can also be put in a glass of water and kept in the refrigerator.

soups, stews, & salads

2

Pumpkin-Ginger Soup
Topped with Crème Fraîche and Condiments

GINGER GIVES THIS SIMPLE PUREED SOUP A SLIGHTLY EXOTIC FLAVOR THAT IS

HIGHLIGHTED BY TOPPINGS OF TANGY CRÈME FRAÎCHE, SLIVERED LEEK, AND CILANTRO.

FOR AN EXTRA-SPECIAL TREATMENT, SERVE IN A PUMPKIN TUREEN (SEE PAGE 36),

WITH THE CONDIMENTS SERVED IN MINI-PUMPKIN BOWLS.

1 cooking pumpkin, about 2 pounds,
cut into quarters, seeded, and peeled (see page 12)

3 tablespoons butter

2 large leeks, including 1-inch pale green leaves,
cut into 1/2-inch-thick slices

6 cups chicken broth

2-1/2-inch piece fresh ginger, peeled and minced
to make 1 tablespoon

1/2 teaspoon salt

1/2 teaspoon freshly ground black pepper

CONDIMENTS

1/2 cup crème fraîche

1/2 cup chopped fresh cilantro

Steam the pumpkin until it is tender but still offers a little resistance when pierced with a fork, about 15 minutes. Using a melon baller, scoop the pumpkin flesh into balls and set aside.

In a soup pot, melt the butter over medium heat. Add all but 2 of the leek slices and sauté for 2 or 3 minutes, or until nearly translucent. Add the broth, minced ginger, salt, pepper, and pumpkin balls. Bring to just below a boil, then reduce heat.

Simmer until the pumpkin is very tender, about 10 minutes.

To prepare the condiments, cut the 2 reserved leeks into very thin slices and put them in a small bowl. Put the crème fraîche and the chopped cilantro in separate small bowls.

To serve, ladle the hot soup into bowls, garnish with a spoonful of the crème fraîche, and other condiments as desired. *Serves 6 to 8*

Pumpkin and Black Bean Soup

BEANS AND PUMPKINS ARE A CLASSIC COMBINATION IN ITALY, WHERE THEY
ARE USED IN PASTAS AS WELL AS SOUPS. THIS SOUP HAS A SOUTH-OF-THE-BORDER
FLAVOR, THANKS TO BLACK BEANS AND CHILIES.

1 cup dried black beans

6 cups water

2 teaspoons salt

1 bay leaf

2 tablespoons minced fresh thyme

1 teaspoon dried winter savory

1 or 2 dried Anaheim chiles

1 large cooking pumpkin or 2 smaller ones,
any kind, about 8 to 10 pounds

2 tablespoons butter, cut into bits

1-1/2 cups vegetable or chicken broth

1 teaspoon freshly ground black pepper

2 sweet red peppers, seeded, de-ribbed and
minced for garnish

In a large pot, combine the beans, water, 1 teaspoon of the salt, the bay leaf, thyme, winter savory, and the whole chiles. Bring to a boil, reduce heat to low, and simmer until the beans are tender, about 1-1/2 hours. Drain, reserving the bean broth. Discard the chilies, cover, and set aside.

Preheat the oven to 350°F. Cut the pumpkin into wedges about 3 to 4 inches wide. Scrape out and discard the seeds and their fibers, or save the seeds for toasting (see page 23). Place the pumpkin, cut-side up, on a baking sheet and dot with the butter. Bake until very soft and easily pierced with a knife, about 1-1/2 hours. Let cool to the touch.

Scrape the soft flesh from the skins.

Using a blender or food processor, in batches if necessary, puree the pumpkin with the vegetable or chicken broth and 1 cup of the reserved liquid from the beans. Pour into a soup pot and add the remaining salt and the black pepper. Cook over medium heat, stirring often, until the soup is hot, about 10 minutes. Stir in the beans and cook until the beans are thoroughly hot, about 5 minutes.

To serve, ladle into bowls and garnish with the sweet peppers. *Serves 6 to 8*

Pumpkin Soup Topped with Croutons and Fresh Thyme

BAKED PUMPKIN MAKES A RICH AND FLAVORFUL SOUP WHEN

COMBINED WITH BROTH, MILK, AND SEASONINGS.

1 small cooking pumpkin, about 3 pounds

1 tablespoon plus 2 teaspoons butter

2 leeks, white parts only, finely chopped

2/3 cup water

2/3 cup chicken broth

1-1/3 cups milk

1 teaspoon salt

1 teaspoon pepper

1/2 cup homemade or purchased seasoned croutons

1 teaspoon minced fresh thyme

Preheat the oven to 350°F. Cut off the stem, then cut the pumpkin in half crosswise with a sharp knife. Scoop out and discard the seeds and their fibers or save the seeds for toasting (see page 23).

Rub the cavities and cut edges of each half of the pumpkin with two teaspoons of butter, then place the halves cut-side down on a baking sheet and bake until the pumpkin is very soft and easily pierced with a fork, 1 to 1-1/2 hours. Remove from the oven and scrape the pulp into a bowl, discarding the skin.

In a large, heavy saucepan, melt the remaining tablespoon of butter over medium heat and sauté the leeks until soft, about 6 or 7 minutes. Add the water and chicken broth and simmer for about 15 minutes. Stir in the pumpkin pulp and simmer another 5 minutes. In a blender or food processor, puree the pumpkin mixture and 1/3 cup of the milk. Pour the mixture back into the same saucepan. Stir in the salt, pepper, and remaining 1 cup of milk. Heat until very hot, but not boiling.

Ladle the hot soup into bowls and top with the croutons and thyme. *Serves 4*

Beef and Pumpkin Stew with Pomegranates

PUMPKIN CUBES AND SMOKY GREEN CHILES ARE
COOKED SEPARATELY, THEN ADDED TO THE SIMMERED BEEF
ALONG WITH POMEGRANATE JUICE AND SEEDS TO MAKE
A HEARTY AND FESTIVE DISH.

One 2-pound cooking pumpkin, peeled, seeded,
and cut into 1-inch cubes (see page 12)

3 poblano chiles

1 pomegranate

1 tablespoon olive oil

2 tablespoons butter

2 cloves garlic, crushed

1-1/2 pounds beef chuck roast,
cut into 1-1/2-inch cubes

1 tablespoon flour

1 teaspoon ground turmeric

1/2 teaspoon ground cumin

1/2 teaspoon salt

1/2 teaspoon cayenne pepper

1/2 cup dry red wine

1 cup beef broth

1 cup water

continued next page

21

Steam the pumpkin cubes until just tender, about 15 minutes. Meanwhile, preheat a broiler or gas grill, or light a fire in a charcoal grill. Place the chiles on a broiler pan or grill rack and broil or grill until the skins are charred and blistered, 2 to 3 minutes on each side. Transfer the chiles to a plastic bag, close it, and let them sweat for about 5 minutes. Remove from the bag and slit lengthwise. Remove the stems and seeds, and using your fingers, peel off the skins. Cut the chiles lengthwise into 1/2-inch-wide strips and set aside.

Cut the pomegranate into halves and, using your fingers, remove enough of the seeds to measure 1/4 cup. Using a juice extractor or reamer, juice the pomegranate halves. Strain the juice to remove any bits of the bitter white pith. Set the seeds and juice aside.

In a deep, heavy saucepan over medium heat, heat the olive oil and 1 tablespoon of the butter. Add the garlic and sauté for a minute or two. Add the beef and sauté, stirring often, until browned on all sides, about 7 or 8 minutes.

Sprinkle the flour, turmeric, cumin, 1/4 teaspoon of the salt, and 1/4 teaspoon of the cayenne over the meat. Stir the meat to brown the flour and spices, about 3 to 4 minutes. Add the red wine and stir to scrape up any browned bits on the bottom of the pan. Add the beef broth and water, reduce heat to low, and simmer until the beef is fork-tender, 1-1/2 to 2 hours.

While the stew is cooking, melt the remaining butter in a skillet over medium heat. Add the pumpkin and increase heat to medium high. Sprinkle with the remaining 1/4 teaspoon salt and 1/4 teaspoon cayenne, and sauté until browned, about 5 to 7 minutes. Remove and set aside.

When the meat is tender, add the pumpkin, chile strips, and pomegranate juice. Simmer for about 5 minutes, then serve, topping each serving with a sprinkling of the pomegranate seeds. *Serves 4 to 6*

Roasted Pumpkin Seeds

THESE CRUNCHY ROASTED SEEDS, CALLED *PEPITAS* IN MEXICO,
WHERE THEY ARE OFTEN SERVED AS AN HORS D'OEUVRE, CAN BE EATEN WITHOUT
SHELLING, AS THE SHELL BECOMES NICELY CRISP DURING COOKING.

2 tablespoons canola or light vegetable oil

1 cup seeds from any freshly cut pumpkin,
washed and dried

Salt to taste

Preheat the oven to 325°F. In a skillet over medium high heat, heat the oil. When the oil is hot, sauté the seeds, stirring frequently until lightly browned, about 5 minutes. Using a slotted spoon, transfer the seeds to an ungreased baking sheet and spread them into a single layer. Sprinkle with salt and bake until crisp, about 15 minutes.

Using the slotted spoon, transfer the seeds to paper towels and let cool. Store in an airtight container for up to 1 month. *Makes about 1 cup*

Spinach and Pumpkin Seed Salad

SHELLED PUMPKIN SEEDS ADD AN INVITING TEXTURE

AND FLAVOR TO THIS HEALTHFUL SALAD.

1/4 cup extra-virgin olive oil

3 tablespoons red wine vinegar

1/2 teaspoon salt

1/2 teaspoon freshly ground
black pepper

1/2 teaspoon Dijon mustard

5 cups stemmed spinach leaves,
washed and dried

1 cup cherry tomatoes,
red and yellow, if possible

1/4 cup finely chopped
green onions, including 1 inch
of their green stems

1 cup alfalfa sprouts

1/2 cup shelled pumpkin seeds
(available at the supermarket)

In a salad bowl, combine the olive oil and the vinegar, stirring them together with a fork. Add the salt, pepper, and mustard and stir to mix well. Add the spinach leaves and toss them in the dressing until well coated. Add the tomatoes and onions and toss again. Add the alfalfa sprouts, tossing them once or twice, then sprinkle the pumpkin seeds over the salad and serve. *Serves 4 to 5*

Frisée Salad with Deep-Fried Pumpkin Bits and Lardons

GOLDEN ORANGE PUMPKIN BITS AND DEEP BROWN LARDONS GIVE THIS SALAD A FESTIVE FALL COLOR AND FLAVOR.

1/2 cup all-purpose flour

1/4 teaspoon salt

1/4 teaspoon freshly ground
black pepper

1/2 teaspoon dried thyme leaves

1 cup 1/4-inch-diced pumpkin

Oil for frying

2 slices thick bacon,
cut into 1/4-inch-thick pieces

VINAIGRETTE

1/4 cup extra-virgin olive oil

1/4 cup balsamic vinegar

1 clove garlic, minced

1/4 teaspoon salt

1/4 teaspoon freshly ground pepper

4 cups frisée (curly endive),
pale inner leaves only,
about 2 large heads or 4 small

In a large bowl, mix together the flour, salt, pepper, and thyme. Coat the diced pumpkin in the flour mixture. In a large skillet, heat about 1 inch of oil until a piece of pumpkin dropped in the oil bubbles and sizzles. Add half the pumpkin to the oil and cook for about 3 minutes, stirring constantly. Using a slotted spoon, transfer to paper towels to drain. Repeat with the remaining pumpkin. Keep pumpkin warm in an oven set at a low temperature until ready to assemble the salad.

In a medium skillet, fry the bacon until crisp and brown, about 5 minutes. Using a slotted spoon, transfer to paper towels to drain.

Combine all the vinaigrette ingredients in a salad bowl and mix together with a fork until well blended. Add the frisée and toss well to coat. Divide the frisée equally among 4 warm salad plates. Top each serving with an equal amount of the pumpkin and bacon and serve at once. *Serves 4*

Butterhead Lettuce and Pumpkin Blossom Salad

BRIGHT, GOLDEN PUMPKIN OR SQUASH BLOSSOMS MAKE
A SPRIGHTLY CONTRAST TO THE DELICATE PALE LEAVES OF THE LETTUCE.

1/4 cup extra-virgin olive oil

3 tablespoons Champagne vinegar

2 tablespoons minced shallots

1/2 teaspoon salt

1 teaspoon Dijon mustard

1/2 teaspoon finely ground black pepper

1 head butterhead lettuce, leaves separated

4 pumpkin or squash blossoms (see page 12)

In a salad bowl, combine the olive oil and vinegar, stirring them together with a fork. Add the shallots, salt, pepper, and mustard and stir to mix well. Set aside.

Reserve the dark green exterior lettuce leaves for another use. Tear the light-colored leaves into bite-sized pieces, leaving intact the very small leaves from the innermost heart.

Put the leaves in the bowl with the dressing and toss them until well coated. With scissors, snip the pumpkin blossoms into slivers and add 3/4 of them to the bowl, turning them once or twice with the salad. Sprinkle the remaining slivers across the top of the salad and serve. *Serves 3 to 4*

Root Vegetable and Pumpkin Ragout

BOTH ROOT VEGETABLES AND PUMPKINS ARE IN SEASON IN FALL AND WINTER,
AND THEY SHARE SIMILAR TEXTURES AND FLAVORS. COMBINED TOGETHER IN A FRENCH-STYLE STEW,
THEY MAKE A SUBSTANTIAL MEATLESS MAIN DISH.

4 parsnips, about 1-1/2 pounds total, peeled

2 turnips, about 1 pound total, peeled

2 rutabagas, about 1 pound total, peeled

2 carrots, about 1 pound total, peeled

4 to 5 large chard leaves

3 tablespoons butter

1 tablespoon plus 1/4 cup extra-virgin olive oil

2 yellow onions, quartered

2 tablespoons flour

1 teaspoon salt

1 teaspoon freshly ground black pepper

1 teaspoon ground turmeric

1/3 cup dry white wine

2 cups vegetable broth

1 cup water

1/4 cup raisins

1 cooking pumpkin, about 3 pounds,
peeled, seeded, and cut into 1-inch cubes
(see page 12)

1/4 cup minced fresh chives

2 tablespoons minced fresh parsley

Preheat an oven to 350°F. Cut the parsnips, turnips, and rutabagas into quarters, then halve the quarters to make 8 wedges for each vegetable. Cut the carrots into 1-inch-long pieces.

Cut out the white ribs from the chard and finely chop them. Cut the green part into thin strips by rolling the leaves lengthwise into a thin cigar shape, then cutting across them to make 1/8-inch slivers.

In a Dutch oven or flameproof casserole dish over medium heat, melt the butter with 1 tablespoon of the olive oil. When the mixture foams, add the parsnips, turnips, rutabagas, carrots, and onions. Sauté for 5 to 6 minutes, stirring frequently.

Mix the flour, 1/2 teaspoon of the salt, 1/2 teaspoon of the pepper and the turmeric, and sprinkle the mixture over the vegetables. Cook, stirring frequently, until the flour mixture begins to brown, 3 to 4 minutes. Add the wine and stir for a minute or two. Add the broth, water, half the green chard, the finely chopped white chard, and the raisins. Cover and bake until the vegetables are tender when pierced with a fork, about 1 hour.

Toss the pumpkin cubes, 1/4 cup olive oil, remaining 1/2 teaspoon salt and remaining 1/2 teaspoon pepper together in a bowl. Spread the cubes in a single layer on a baking sheet and bake until tender when pierced with a fork, about 45 minutes.

To assemble, remove the casserole from the oven and stir in the cooked pumpkin cubes and remaining green chard. In a small bowl, combine the chopped chives and parsley. Top each serving of ragout with a generous spoonful of mixed herbs and serve warm. *Serves 6 to 8*

tabletop pumpkins

3

Pumpkin Place Cards

PUMPKINS PAINTED WITH PARTY-GOERS' NAMES CREATE A PERSONAL,

YET FUN AND INFORMAL LOOK FOR A PARTY TABLE.

YOU WILL NEED:

Mini pumpkins

Black fine-pointed ballpoint pen

Black brush-point marker (Niji brand "Instabrush,"
available at art supply stores)

Spray fixative (optional)

TO MAKE:

In a curly script, using the ballpoint pen, write each name several times to make a ring around each pumpkin. (Erase errors with a damp tissue.) Retrace the name outlines with the brush marker, adding thicker strokes where desired. Avoid touching areas of lettering while finishing the script to prevent smearing.

Spray with fixative to make the lettering permanent, if you like.

Place a pumpkin at each setting on your holiday table so that each guest can take one home as a memento of the event.

Pumpkin Candle Holders

CANDLELIGHT ALWAYS SETS A MOOD AND
A SPECIAL TONE FOR A TABLE SETTING, AND CANDLE
HOLDERS OF PUMPKINS IN DIFFERENT COLORS AND
SHAPES LEND A HOLIDAY SPIRIT AS WELL.

YOU WILL NEED:

Assorted pumpkins, squash, or gourds

Garden clippers

Assorted candles, tapers, and votives

Ballpoint pen

X-Acto knife

Glue gun and glue (optional)

TO MAKE:

Remove the pumpkin stems with garden clippers, or leave stems on if desired. With the pen, trace the outlines of the candle bottoms onto the top of the pumpkins.

With an X-Acto knife, hollow out the candle marks 1/2 inch deep for tapers and 3/4 inch deep for votives.

To make a stacked pumpkin candelabra, use pumpkins with straight stems for the bottom tiers, inserting them in holes made in the bottom of the pumpkins in the upper tiers. Alternatively, remove the stems on the lower pumpkins and glue the tiers together.

Insert the candles in the top holes. The pumpkins will last about 4 to 5 days after the holes have been cut.

Pumpkin Soup Tureen with Mini-Pumpkin Condiment Bowls

ELEGANT SOUP TUREENS AND BOWLS ARE EASILY MADE BY

HOLLOWING OUT PUMPKINS. YOU CAN ALTER THE LOOK BY USING PUMPKINS IN VARIED COLORS.

USE THESE PUMPKINS AS CONTAINERS FOR THE SOUP AND CONDIMENTS ON PAGE 16.

YOU WILL NEED:

1 large pumpkin for tureen

3 mini pumpkins for bowls

Marking pen

Large knife

Small knife

Large metal spoon

Small metal spoon

36

TO MAKE:

With the marking pen, draw a scalloped line around the top of the large pumpkin, about 4 inches away from the stem.

Draw a scalloped line around the top of each of the mini pumpkins about 2 inches away from the stem.

With the tip of the large knife, cut through the large pumpkin into the cavity at a spot on the line.

Following the line, cut off the top, and scrape off any fibers.

Using the large metal spoon, scoop out the seeds and fibers from the inside of the pumpkin and discard.

Using the small knife and the small spoon, do the same with the mini pumpkins.

Fill the soup tureen with hot soup and the mini pumpkins with condiments for the soup.

The tureens and bowls should be used the day they are made and will last for one occasion.

White Pumpkin Centerpiece

PUMPKINS OF ALL SHAPES AND SIZES ARE EASILY COMBINED
WITH OTHER FRUITS AND VEGETABLES TO MAKE A DRAMATIC CENTERPIECE
FOR A TABLE OR BUFFET SIDEBOARD.

YOU WILL NEED:

6 to 7 green hydrangeas

6 to 7 water tubes (available from florists)

3 white pumpkins of different sizes

4 to 5 small white gourds

4 to 5 Osage oranges

3 to 4 heads of kale

TO MAKE:

Slit the hydrangea stems from the bottom up about 1 inch and insert them in filled water tubes.

Arrange the pumpkins, gourds, and oranges in a random fashion, then insert the kale and water-tubed flower heads among the pumpkin clusters.

Green Pumpkin Centerpiece

YOU WILL NEED:

Several grapevine lengths,
either fresh or dried

1 large green pumpkin

Several small green pumpkins

Grape clusters

Figs

Other green or purple fruit,
such as apples, plums, or pears

TO MAKE:

Lay some of the grapevine out on the tabletop in a loose star shape. Arrange the pumpkins and fruit on top, adding additional vines over and around the pumpkins as desired.

Cornucopia Centerpiece

YOU WILL NEED:

Cornucopia basket, rustic and sturdy looking

Bittersweet branches

Gourds

Small or mini-pumpkins

Rose hips

Pomegranates

Persimmons with leaves

TO MAKE:

Put the cornucopia on the tabletop. Put the larger branches in first, then insert the other items around them as if everything is spilling out of the cornucopia.

Pumpkin Vase

FLOWERS, SHRUBS, AND FRUITS CAN BE ARRANGED
IN A HOLLOWED-OUT PUMPKIN VASE. THE LONGEVITY
OF THE VASE DEPENDS ON WHETHER YOU FIT
THE PUMPKIN WITH A JAR FOR WATER OR SIMPLY PUT
THE WATER IN THE PUMPKIN ITSELF.

YOU WILL NEED:

1 large pumpkin

Marking pen

Large knife

Large metal spoon

Jar to fit inside pumpkin (optional)

Seasonal flowers

TO MAKE:

With the marking pen, draw a line around the top of the
pumpkin to make a circle 2 inches from the stem.

With the tip of the large knife, cut through the pumpkin
into the cavity at a spot on the line.

Following the line, cut off the top, and scrape off all fibers.

Using the metal spoon, scoop out the seeds and fibers
from the inside of the pumpkin and discard.

Choose a jar that fits inside the pumpkin. Fill it with
water and arrange the flowers in it. Or if desired, simply fill the
pumpkin itself with water and then arrange the flowers.

With a jar of water, the vase will last several days. Otherwise, count on using the vase for only a single day, perhaps two.

grills & savories

4

Honey-Grilled Pumpkin Slices

STEAMED PUMPKIN SLICES, BASTED WITH A MIXTURE OF HONEY AND MUSTARD,

THEN GRILLED AND GARNISHED WITH POMEGRANATE SEEDS, MAKE A TOOTHSOME SIDE DISH

TO ACCOMPANY A MAIN DISH OF ROASTED OR GRILLED MEAT. THEY ARE ESPECIALLY GOOD

WITH PORK OR GAME OR AS PART OF A MIXED VEGETABLE GRILL.

One 2-pound unpeeled cooking pumpkin,
seeded and cut into 1-inch-wide slices

1/2 cup (1 stick) butter, melted

1 teaspoon salt

1 teaspoon freshly ground black pepper

2 tablespoons honey

2 tablespoons Dijon mustard

Pomegranate seeds for garnish

Light a fire in a charcoal or wood grill or preheat a gas grill. Steam the pumpkin slices until tender when pierced with a knife, about 15 minutes (see page 12). Dip the pumpkin slices in the melted butter and place them on a baking sheet. Sprinkle with the salt and pepper. Blend the honey and mustard together into a paste.

Grill the pumpkin slices over medium-hot fire for 2 to 3 minutes on one side. Turn and baste with the honey and mustard mixture. Grill for 2 or 3 minutes more, then turn and baste again. Cook until lightly golden on the bottom, 1 or 2 minutes. Turn and grill on the second side until lightly golden as well, 1 or 2 minutes. Serve hot, sprinkled with pomegranate seeds. *Makes about 15 slices; serves 6 as a side dish*

Sautéed Pumpkin, Red Peppers, and Greens with Polenta

RICH, CREAMY POLENTA IS A PERFECT FOIL FOR SWEET-SHARP GREENS,
TENDER PUMPKIN, AND SWEET PEPPERS. SERVE THIS VEGETARIAN DISH AS A MAIN COURSE, ACCOMPANIED BY
A GREEN SALAD AND LOTS OF CRUSTY FRENCH BREAD FOR A SIMPLE FALL MEAL.

6 cups water

2-3/4 teaspoons salt

1 cup polenta

2 cups 1/2-inch-diced cooking pumpkin, peeled

2 tablespoons olive oil

2 cloves garlic, minced

3/4 teaspoon freshly ground black pepper

2 red bell peppers, seeded, de-ribbed, and
cut into 1-inch pieces

2 bunches spinach, stemmed

2 bunches Swiss chard, white ribs cut out

· 1/4 cup vegetable broth

4 ounces Gorgonzola cheese

3 tablespoons butter

In a heavy, medium saucepan, bring the water and 2 teaspoons of the salt to a boil. Slowly pour in the polenta in a steady stream, whisking constantly. Reduce heat to low and cook for about 40 to 45 minutes, stirring often. The polenta is done when it pulls away slightly from the sides of the pan.

About 20 minutes before the polenta is done, steam the diced pumpkin for about 10 minutes, or until just tender when pierced with a knife (see page 12). In a large skillet or wok over medium-high heat, heat the olive oil and sauté the garlic for 1 or 2 minutes. Add the diced pumpkin and sauté until slightly browned, 4 to 5 minutes. Sprinkle with

1/4 teaspoon each salt and pepper. Using a slotted spoon, transfer to a plate. Sauté the red peppers until limp, 5 or 6 minutes. Add the spinach and chard leaves and sauté until they are limp and tender, yet still bright green, 4 to 5 minutes. Add the broth and 1/4 teaspoon each salt and pepper, and return the pumpkin to the pan. Cook another minute or two. Stir in the cheese, butter, and the remaining 1/4 teaspoon each salt and pepper. Stir to mix well.

To serve, spoon the polenta onto a platter and top it with the mixture of greens, pumpkin, and peppers. *Serves 4 as a main course*

Pumpkin and Chanterelle Mushroom Risotto

RISOTTO, FLECKED WITH PUMPKIN AND MUSHROOMS, MAKES A DELECTABLE,
SAVORY DISH TO SERVE AS A MAIN COURSE OR AS AN ACCOMPANIMENT TO ROAST MEATS SUCH AS
PORK OR BEEF. A GREEN SALAD AND A SIMPLE DESSERT COMPLETE THE MENU.

One 2-pound cooking pumpkin, seeded and
cut into 3-inch-thick slices

2-1/2 cups chicken broth

2-1/2 cups water

5 tablespoons butter

2 tablespoons olive oil

2 tablespoons finely chopped onion

1-1/2 cups Arborio rice

6 ounces chanterelle mushrooms, coarsely chopped

1 teaspoon salt

1 teaspoon freshly ground black pepper

1 teaspoon minced fresh thyme

1/4 cup freshly grated Parmesan cheese

2 tablespoons minced fresh parsley

Steam the pumpkin slices until tender, about 15 minutes. Peel and discard the pumpkin skin and cut the flesh into 1/4-inch dice. You should have about 1 cup. Set aside.

In a large saucepan, bring the broth and water to a boil over high heat. Reduce heat to low and let simmer.

In a large, heavy saucepan, melt 3 tablespoons of the butter and the olive oil over medium heat and sauté the onion until translucent, 2 to 3 minutes. Add the rice and stir until shiny and opaque, 2 to 3 minutes. Add 3/4 cup of the broth mixture to the rice and stir. Reduce heat to low and cook, stirring frequently, until the rice has absorbed the liquid. Continue this process until the rice is al dente and has absorbed all but the last 1/2 cup, 15 to 20 minutes.

While the rice is cooking, melt 1 tablespoon of butter in a medium skillet and add the mushrooms and pumpkin. Sprinkle with 1/2 teaspoon each of salt and pepper. Sauté just until the mushrooms are limp and cooked through, and the pumpkin is slightly golden, 4 to 5 minutes. Set aside.

Stir into the rice the Parmesan cheese, the remaining tablespoon of butter, and 1/2 teaspoon each of salt and pepper. Stir in the pumpkin and mushrooms and the remaining broth mixture. Stir constantly until the risotto is creamy, 4 to 5 minutes. Sprinkle with the parsley, spoon onto plates, and serve immediately. *Serves 3 as a main course, 4 to 5 as a first course or side dish*

Pumpkin Pasta with Baby Bok Choy, Prosciutto, and Pecans

PUMPKIN CONTRIBUTES COLOR AND FLAVOR TO HOMEMADE PASTA,

A BEAUTIFUL BACKGROUND FOR THE ASSERTIVE TOPPINGS.

PASTA DOUGH

1/4 cup homemade or canned
pumpkin puree

2 cups all-purpose flour

1 teaspoon salt

1 egg

3 tablespoons butter

1/4 teaspoon freshly ground black pepper

4 baby bok choy, cut lengthwise
into 1/2-inch-thick slices

1/2 cup pecans, coarsely chopped

4 ounces thinly sliced prosciutto or
Virginia ham, cut into slivers

To make the pasta dough: In a food processor, combine all the ingredients and process until a ball forms, about 1 minute. To make by hand, mix all the ingredients in a bowl with a wooden spoon. On a lightly floured board, knead the dough until smooth, about 5 minutes.

By hand or using a pasta machine, roll the dough into sheets about 1/8 inch thick. Cut into strips about 1/4 inch wide.

In a large pot of salted water, cook the pasta until tender, 3 or 4 minutes. Drain and transfer to a heated serving platter.

Add 1 tablespoon butter and the black pepper and toss. Set aside and keep warm.

In a skillet, heat 2 tablespoons butter over medium-high heat and sauté the bok choy until wilted, about 3 minutes. Using a slotted spoon, transfer the bok choy to the pasta. In the same pan, sauté the pecans and prosciutto or ham for about 30 seconds. Add more butter if necessary. Stir the bok choy and half the pecan mixture into the pasta. Garnish with the remaining pecan mixture and serve hot. *Serves 4 as a main course*

Scalloped Pumpkin and Potatoes

POTATOES AND PUMPKIN, BAKED SLOWLY IN MILK AND CHEESE

AND FAINTLY FLAVORED WITH GARLIC, MAKE A DELICIOUS GRATIN TO ACCOMPANY

A MAIN COURSE SUCH AS ROAST TURKEY OR A STANDING RIB ROAST.

1/2 small cooking pumpkin, seeded,
cut into wedges, and steamed (see page 12)

1 clove garlic, crushed

4 tablespoons butter, cut into bits

1-1/2 pounds boiling potatoes, such as red
or white rose or Yukon gold, peeled and cut into
1/8-inch-thick slices, 5 to 6 cups

1 teaspoon salt

1/2 teaspoon freshly ground black pepper

1 cup (4 ounces) grated Swiss cheese

1 cup milk, boiling

Preheat the oven to 425°F. Peel the steamed wedges of pumpkin and cut them crosswise into 1/8-inch-thick slices; you should have 2 cups. Reserve any extra pumpkin for another use.

Rub the inside of a shallow baking dish with the garlic, then liberally butter the dish. Arrange half the potato slices in the bottom of the dish, add half the sliced pumpkin, then top with half the salt, pepper, cheese, and butter. Repeat the layering a second time. Pour in the boiling milk. Bake until the potatoes and pumpkin are thoroughly tender and the top is browned, 40 to 45 minutes. *Serves 6 as a side dish*

Pumpkins and Mixed Winter Squash Filled with Savory Puree

SEVERAL DIFFERENT KINDS OF WINTER SQUASHES AND PUMPKINS ARE PUREED, SEASONED, HEAPED BACK INTO THEIR SHELLS, AND THEN BAKED. A MIXTURE OF SHAPES, SIZES, AND COLORS CREATES AN ENTICING ARRAY.

2 ounces pancetta or bacon, cut into 1/4-inch pieces

2 mini pumpkins

2 Sweet Dumpling squash

2 acorn squash

1 small butternut squash

1 large butternut squash

1 Delicata squash

1 teaspoon dried thyme

1/2 teaspoon salt

1/2 teaspoon freshly ground black pepper

2 tablespoons butter, melted,
plus 1 tablespoon butter cut into bits

1/2 cup nonfat sour cream

1/4 cup freshly grated Parmesan cheese

Preheat the oven to 350°F. In a medium skillet, over medium-high heat, fry the pancetta or bacon until crisp. Using a slotted spoon, transfer to paper towels to drain.

Place the pumpkins and squash on a baking sheet and bake until they are easily pierced with a knife, about 1 hour to 1 hour and 15 minutes. The larger butternut squash may take another 15 to 20 minutes. Remove from the oven, and let cool to the touch.

Cut the upper fourth from the mini pumpkins and Sweet Dumpling squash. Cut the acorn, Delicata, and butternut squash in half lengthwise. Scoop out and discard the seeds and fibers. Using a large metal spoon, make shells from the mini pumpkins and the acorn, Delicata, and small butternut squash by scooping out all but about 1/4 inch of the flesh. Put the flesh in a bowl. Scoop out the flesh from the upper portions of the Sweet Dumpling squash and mini pumpkins and add it to the bowl. Scoop out all the flesh of the large butternut squash and add it to the bowl. You should have about 4 to 5 cups of flesh. Add the thyme, salt and pepper, melted butter, and sour cream. Beat until fluffy. Stir in the fried pancetta or bacon until well blended. Spoon the mixture into the squash shells, swirling the filling above the rim of the squash. Sprinkle with the grated cheese and dot with the bits of butter. Increase the oven temperature to 375°F. Bake until thoroughly hot and lightly golden on top, about 20 minutes. Serve hot. *Serves 8 as a side dish or 4 to 6 as a main course*

Pumpkin Blossoms with Goat Cheese Filling

PUMPKIN AND SQUASH BLOSSOMS MAKE BEAUTIFUL, DELICATELY
FLAVORED CONTAINERS FOR STUFFING. HERE, THEY ARE FILLED WITH SOFT GOAT CHEESE,
SEASONED WITH HERBS, THEN COOKED IN A LIGHT TOMATO SAUCE.

8 ounces fresh goat cheese at room temperature

1-1/4 teaspoon freshly ground black pepper

1-1/4 teaspoon salt

3 tablespoons minced fresh thyme

8 pumpkin or other squash blossoms, stemmed
(see page 12)

1 tablespoon butter

1 tablespoon olive oil

2 tablespoons minced shallots

8 ounces canned Italian plum tomatoes, drained and
finely chopped, the juice reserved

In a medium bowl, combine the cheese, 1/2 teaspoon of the pepper, 1/2 teaspoon of the salt, and 2 tablespoons of the thyme. Mix well. Fill each blossom by gently opening it and spooning in about 1-1/2 tablespoons of the cheese mixture; it should reach nearly to the point on the blossom where the petals begin to separate into points. Fold the points over the filling, overlapping them. Gently close the fold with a toothpick. Place stuffed blossoms on a plate upright, folded-side down.

In a large skillet over medium-high heat, melt the butter with the olive oil and sauté the shallots until translucent. Add the tomatoes and the remaining salt, pepper, and thyme. Reduce the heat to low and simmer for about 10 minutes. Add the stuffed blossoms, placing them folded-side down in the skillet. Increase heat to medium, cover, and cook for 3 to 4 minutes. Reduce heat to low and continue to cook for 2 to 3 minutes.

Serve hot or at room temperature accompanied by a spoonful or two of the tomatoes. *Serves 4 as a first course*

Whipped Pumpkin on Caramelized Onions with Spicy Walnuts

A RICH LAYERING OF SWEET AND SPICY TASTES AND DIFFERENT TEXTURES CREATES A DISH OF COMPLEX FLAVORS.

CARAMELIZED ONIONS

3 tablespoons butter, cut into bits

1 pound onions, peeled and sliced 1/4-inch thick

1/2 dried bay leaf, crumbled

1 teaspoon minced fresh thyme

1 teaspoon minced fresh savory leaves, or pinch of dried

1/2 teaspoon freshly ground black pepper

2 tablespoons olive oil

SPICY WALNUTS

1 tablespoon cayenne pepper

1 teaspoon sugar

1/2 teaspoon salt

3 egg whites

1-1/2 cups walnut halves

WHIPPED PUMPKIN

2 tablespoons butter

1 tablespoon honey

4 to 5 cups homemade or canned pumpkin puree

1/2 teaspoon salt

2 tablespoons firmly packed brown sugar

To make the caramelized onions: Preheat the oven to 300°F. Sprinkle the butter on a 10-inch-by-16-inch baking sheet. Put the baking sheet in the oven until the butter is melted, about 3 or 4 minutes, then remove the pan and put the sliced onions on it in a heaping layer. Sprinkle with the bay leaf, herbs and pepper. Drizzle with the olive oil. Bake, stirring the onions every 10 or 15 minutes, until the onions have turned a light golden brown and have reduced in volume by nearly half, 1 to 1-1/2 hours. To prepare in advance, store in an airtight container in the refrigerator for up to a week.

To make the spicy walnuts: Preheat the oven to 225°F. In a small bowl, stir the cayenne pepper, sugar, and salt together. In a large bowl, beat the egg whites until frothy. Using a small paintbrush or your fingertips, lightly coat each walnut half with a small amount of the egg whites and then sprinkle with some of the cayenne mixture, coating both sides. Place the coated walnuts on a baking sheet. Bake until the nuts are toasted, 15 to 20 minutes. Let cool completely. Store in an airtight container in a dry place for up to 3 months. *Makes 1-1/2 cups*

To make the whipped pumpkin: In a large saucepan, heat the butter and honey over medium heat. Add the pumpkin puree, stirring well to mix, then add the salt and brown sugar.

To serve, heat the caramelized onions if necessary. Place a thin layer of warm onions on each warmed plate, top with several spoonfuls of the pumpkin, and garnish with the spicy walnuts. *Serves 4 to 6 as a side dish or first course*

Baked Pumpkins Stuffed with Sausage and Sage

THE SAVORY JUICES OF THE HERBED STUFFING PERMEATE AND FLAVOR THE PUMPKINS AS THEY BAKE,

MAKING A DECORATIVE AND TASTY PRESENTATION FOR A FALL MEAL.

6 mini pumpkins, 2-1/2 to 3 inches in diameter

12 ounces bulk pork sausage

1 egg

1 cup coarse Italian-style, seasoned bread crumbs, homemade or purchased

1 tablespoon minced fresh sage

1 tablespoon minced fresh parsley

1/2 teaspoon freshly ground black pepper

Salt to taste

With a sharp knife, slice off the upper one-fourth of the pumpkins and set the tops aside. Scoop out the seeds, and if necessary, enough flesh to leave a shell about 1/2 inch thick.

Preheat the oven to 350°F. In a medium bowl, combine the sausage, egg, bread crumbs, sage, parsley, pepper, and salt, and mix well. Fill each pumpkin with some of the stuffing, mounding it 1/2 inch above the rim. Place the pumpkins on a baking sheet with their tops alongside, stem up. Bake until the filling is firm and has begun to pull away just slightly from the sides and the pumpkin shells are easily pierced with a knife, 35 to 45 minutes.

Replace the tops and serve hot. *Serves 6 as a first course or side dish*

Grilled Quail with Herbed Mashed Pumpkin

THE SLIGHTLY GAMEY FLAVOR OF QUAIL PAIRS BEAUTIFULLY WITH WELL-SEASONED PUMPKIN.

8 quail

1/4 cup olive oil

2 tablespoons freshly ground black pepper

2 teaspoons salt

1 teaspoon fresh minced sage

HERBED MASHED PUMPKIN

2 tablespoons butter

1/2 teaspoon salt

1/2 teaspoon freshly ground black pepper

1 teaspoon minced fresh sage

1/2 teaspoon minced fresh rosemary

1 teaspoon minced fresh thyme

5 cups homemade or canned pumpkin puree

1/2 cup nonfat sour cream

2 ounces Gorgonzola cheese

Light a fire in a wood or charcoal grill or preheat a broiler. Rub the quail with olive oil. Sprinkle inside and out with the pepper, salt, and sage.

To grill, lightly oil a grill basket and add the quail. Place the grill basket over a medium-hot fire and cook for 4 or 5 minutes, then turn. Repeat twice until a thigh can be readily moved and the juices run clear or slightly pink when a knife is inserted at the base of the thigh, a total of about 20 minutes.

To broil, cook the quail on a broiling pan in the same fashion.

To make the mashed pumpkin: In a double boiler, melt the butter. Add the salt, pepper, sage, rosemary, and thyme, then the pumpkin puree. Cook, stirring frequently, until the pumpkin is hot, 4 or 5 minutes. Stir in the sour cream and cheese, then mash until well blended.

Serve a scoop of mashed pumpkin with each pair of grilled quail. *Serves 4 as a main course*

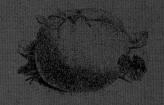

outdoor pumpkins

5

Pumpkin Wreath

PUMPKINS ARE EASILY INCORPORATED INTO A CELEBRATORY, SEASONAL WREATH

BY ATTACHING THEM FIRMLY USING A GLUE GUN AND HOT GLUE.

YOU WILL NEED:

3 to 5 fresh raintree branches
(available at floral suppliers)

Glue gun and glue

12-inch wire wreath frame

13 to 15 orange mini pumpkins,
as small as possible

2 to 3 stems of dried Chinese lantern
(available at floral suppliers)

Wire or ribbon for hanging

TO MAKE:

Remove the raintree blossoms from their branches and glue them on to the wire frame to form the mat. You should have some blossoms left over.

Glue pumpkins directly onto raintree blossoms in varied clusters and angles. Add touches of Chinese lantern.

Add short pieces of raintree branches to the outside of the wreath frame in various spots to create little tendrils, then fill in the wreath with the remaining raintree blossoms to make it look full and to add dimension.

To hang the wreath, attach a piece of ribbon or a twisted wire loop to the back of the wire frame.

Pumpkin Harvest Swag

NO ORNAMENTAL DOOR SWAG COULD BE SIMPLER

TO MAKE THAN THIS CASUAL CLUSTER OF BITTERSWEET BRANCHES ACCENTED

WITH TINY PUMPKINS AND BRILLIANT FALL LEAVES.

YOU WILL NEED:

10 to 15 bittersweet branches of different lengths

Florist tape

Fresh pumpkin vine or soft stem material
like natural-colored raffia

3 to 4 mini pumpkins, the smallest you can find

Fall leaves

Glue gun and glue

Ribbon

TO MAKE:

Place the branches of bittersweet side by side and tape them
firmly at the stem end.

Bind the branches together again at the upper end with
the pumpkin vine or stem material, filling the area where the
pumpkins will be to create a base for them.

Glue the pumpkins on in a cluster on the upper end of
the bittersweet and add leaves to the cluster. Wind the ribbon
around the cluster of pumpkins with loops and twists, gluing
as you go.

Attach a piece of ribbon to the back to hang the swag.

Hanging Mini Monsters

CHILDREN WILL DELIGHT IN THESE SMALL GOBLIN FACES EERILY LIT BY CANDLES AND HUNG FROM BRANCHES, WINDOWS OR PORCH EAVES.

YOU WILL NEED:

Mini pumpkins and gourds

Marking pen

X-Acto knife

Sharp paring knife

Scissors

Large metal spoon and melon baller

Electric drill and large bits (1/4 inch to 3/8 inch)

Twine

Tea lights, removed from their aluminum casings

TO MAKE:

Cut out the top of each pumpkin and gourd and scrape the inside free of seeds and fibers using the metal spoon and melon baller.

Draw a design on each pumpkin and gourd with the marking pen and cut out the design with the X-Acto knife.

Using the drill and a large bit, drill a hole on both sides of each pumpkin and gourd about 1/2 inch below the top to form the holes for hanging the twine. Drill several holes on the back to allow air to feed the candle.

Cut a piece of twine about 2 feet long for each mini monster. Put each end of each piece of twine through one of the two holes in each mini monster from the outside and tie a large knot on each end on the inside. Place a tea light inside.

Replace the tops and hang the mini monsters from branches, posts, or beams, taking care that they are not near anything flammable and monitoring them as you would any jack-o'-lantern lit by candles.

Parchment- or Tissue-Lined Jack-O'-Lanterns

THE SPIRIT OF HALLOWEEN IS EMBODIED
BY JACK-O'-LANTERNS OF ALL KINDS.
TRY MAKING A WHOLE STRING OF THESE
SPECIAL ONES, WHICH HAVE A SPOOKY
LIGHTING EFFECT DUE TO THEIR
PARCHMENT PAPER OR TISSUE LINING.

YOU WILL NEED:

1 or more pumpkins

Large metal spoon, melon baller (optional)

Pen or pencil

Sheet of paper for a template

Scissors

Sharp paring knife and wood-carving tools

X-Acto knife

Parchment paper or tissue paper

Masking tape

Thumbtacks

String of large outdoor Christmas lights

Electrical tape

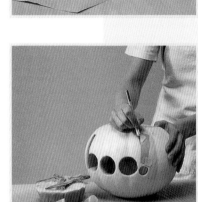

TO MAKE:

STEP 1 Cut out the top and scoop out the cavity of each pumpkin. Create a template by drawing letters or a funny face on the paper. Tape the cutout letters or design onto the pumpkin.

STEP 2 Trace the edges of the word or design with the X-Acto knife. Cut along the traced lines with the paring knife and wood-carving tools and remove the cut pieces from the pumpkin.

STEP 3 Trace the template on the paper. Draw smaller circles inside the centers of the circular part of the letters or the face and cut only the innermost circles. Attach the parchment or tissue paper to the inner walls of the pumpkin with thumbtacks, centering the cutouts in the paper over the holes cut in the pumpkin.

STEP 4 Cut a small hole in the bottom of the pumpkin just large enough for a Christmas light to pass through and draw a light up through the bottom. To create a string of pumpkins, repeat with other cut and lined pumpkins. Remove any unused light bulbs in the string, tape the empty sockets over firmly with electrical tape, and plug in.

Wood-Carving Jack-O'-Lanterns

THESE UNUSUAL, HIGH-DESIGN JACK-O'-LANTERNS HAVE STRIKING LIGHTING PATTERNS BECAUSE
THE GLOWING, ACCENTED AREAS SET OFF THE DIRECT LIGHT OF THE CUTOUTS.

YOU WILL NEED:

1 large pumpkin

Pen

Large carving knife

Large metal spoon

Paper

Masking tape

X-Acto knife

Sharp paring knife

Wood-carver's tools (available at art supply stores)

Melon baller

Votive candle

TO MAKE:

With the pen, draw a line around the top of the pumpkin about 4 inches away from the stem.

With the tip of the large knife, cut through the pumpkin into the cavity at a spot on the line. Following the line, cut off the top and scrape off any fibers.

Using the spoon, scoop out the seeds and fibers from the inside of the pumpkin and discard.

Make a paper template of your design, cut it out, and tape it to the pumpkin.

Trace around the design on the pumpkin with the X-Acto knife and cut out the desired area with the paring knife.

Create an additional contrast to the cutouts by using the wood-carver's tools to remove only the skin in the remaining traced areas. Then, working from the inside with the melon baller, thin out the flesh so that the light will shine through. You may have to test it several times with the candle in a dark place.

When you are satisfied with your carving and thinning of the pumpkin, place the votive candle in it and light it.

pumpkin desserts

6

Pumpkin Cheesecake
in a Gingersnap-Walnut Crust

THE FULL FLAVOR OF THE PUMPKIN AND FRESHLY GROUND SPICES ARE ENHANCED BY THE SPICY GINGERSNAPS.

GINGERSNAP-WALNUT CRUST

6 ounces gingersnap cookies, finely ground,
to make 2-1/2 cups

4 to 5 ounces walnuts, finely ground,
to make 3/4 cup

1/4 cup granulated sugar

4 to 5 tablespoons butter, melted

FILLING

Two 8-ounce packages cream cheese
at room temperature

3/4 cup firmly packed brown sugar

2 eggs

3-1/3 cups homemade or canned
pumpkin puree

1/2 cup heavy cream

1/2 teaspoon freshly ground mace

1/2 teaspoon freshly ground ginger

1/2 teaspoon freshly grated nutmeg

1 teaspoon freshly ground cinnamon

Preheat the oven to 325°F. In a small bowl, mix the ground cookies, walnuts, granulated sugar, and melted butter. Press the mixture over the bottom of a 9-by-2-1/2-inch round springform pan. Using your fingertips, push all but a thin coating of the cookie mixture toward the sides of the pan. Pressing with your fingertips, make a crust about 1-1/2 inches up the sides of the pan; the edges will be slightly irregular.

Bake until lightly browned, about 15 minutes. Let cool thoroughly in the refrigerator before filling.

To make the filling: In a large bowl, using an electric mixer, beat the cream cheese and brown sugar together until well blended. Beat in the eggs, one at a time, until the mixture is smooth and uniform.

In a medium bowl, using a spoon, mix the pumpkin puree, cream, and spices together until well blended. Add the pumpkin mixture to the cream cheese mixture, mixing until well blended. Pour the filling into the crust and bake for about 50 minutes, or until the center barely moves when jiggled.

Let cool on a wire rack, then refrigerate at least overnight before serving. To serve, run a knife around the edge of the pan, then release the sides, leaving the bottom of the pan in place. Serve chilled. *Serves 12*

Pumpkin-Filled Phyllo Cups

DELICATE, CRISPY, GOLDEN PHYLLO CUPS ARE FILLED WITH A MIXTURE OF SWEETENED AND SPICED RICOTTA CHEESE AND PUMPKIN, THEN TOPPED WITH WHIPPED CREAM AND CANDIED GINGER FOR AN ELEGANT BUT SIMPLE SWEET.

4 sheets frozen phyllo dough, thawed

4 tablespoons butter, melted

PUMPKIN FILLING

2 teaspoons plain gelatin

1/2 cup cold 2% milk

1/2 cup warm whole milk

1 tablespoon cold espresso or strong coffee

1 cup low-fat ricotta cheese

1 cup homemade or canned pumpkin puree

1/2 cup firmly packed brown sugar

1/2 teaspoon ground cinnamon

1/2 teaspoon grated nutmeg

1/2 teaspoon ground ginger

1/4 teaspoon salt

1 teaspoon vanilla extract

Whipped cream for serving

1/2 cup candied ginger, chopped, for garnish

Preheat the oven to 325°F. Butter 12 muffin cups. Lay 1 sheet of the phyllo dough on a piece of waxed paper or aluminum foil and brush thoroughly with some of the melted butter. (Keep the other sheets covered with a damp cloth to prevent them from drying out.) Repeat, stacking and buttering the remaining phyllo on top of the first sheet. Cut the stack into 12 squares. Tuck each square into a muffin cup. Bake until golden and crisp, 25 to 30 minutes. Let cool.

To make the filling: Sprinkle the gelatin over the cold milk and let stand for 3 or 4 minutes. In a blender or food processor combine the gelatin mixture, warm milk, espresso or coffee, ricotta, pumpkin puree, brown sugar, cinnamon, nutmeg, ginger, salt, and vanilla. Process until well mixed, about 45 seconds to 1 minute. Pour into a shallow baking dish and chill at least 1 hour and up to 12 hours. Spoon into the phyllo cups. Serve topped with whipped cream and candied ginger. *Makes 12 servings*

Pumpkin Flan

PUMPKIN PUREE AND HEADY, FRESHLY GROUND SPICES MAKE A FLAN LIKE A CRUSTLESS PUMPKIN PIE TOPPED WITH A DELICATE EGG CUSTARD. THE PUMPKIN AND THE CUSTARD SEPARATE DURING COOKING, AND WHEN THE FLAN IS TURNED OUT ON A SERVING PLATE, THE CUSTARD IS THE UPPER LAYER, THE PUMPKIN THE LOWER. THE COMBINATION OF TEXTURES AND FLAVORS IS EXQUISITE.

1 cup milk

2 cups heavy cream

6 eggs

1 cup sugar

1/2 teaspoon salt

1 teaspoon freshly ground cinnamon

1/2 teaspoon freshly ground cloves

1 teaspoon finely grated fresh ginger

1 teaspoon vanilla extract

3/4 cup homemade or canned pumpkin puree

Preheat the oven to 325°F. Butter a 10-inch-by-1-1/2-inch straight-sided, round glass or ceramic cake pan or flan mold. In a medium saucepan, heat the milk and cream together over medium heat until bubbles form around the edges of the pan. At the same time, bring a kettle of water to a boil.

In a large bowl, beat the eggs lightly. Add the sugar, salt, spices, ginger, vanilla, and pumpkin puree and stir to blend well. When the milk mixture is ready, slowly pour it into the egg mixture, stirring constantly until well mixed. Place the prepared cake dish in a shallow roasting pan. Pour the custard mixture into the cake dish; it should fill the dish almost to the rim. Pour the boiling water into the roasting pan to reach halfway up the sides of the cake dish. Bake the flan until it is puffed and golden and a knife inserted in the center comes out clean, 45 to 50 minutes. Remove the flan from the water-filled roasting pan and let it cool to room temperature.

To unmold the flan, slide a thin-bladed knife or spatula around the edge of the pan to loosen it. Invert a shallow serving plate on top of the flan, and holding the flan and serving plate firmly together, turn them back over. The flan pan will now be on top and should lift off easily. Serve warm, at room temperature, or chilled. *Makes 8 to 10 servings*

Harvest Pie

A SIMPLE PUMPKIN PIE IS GIVEN A SURPRISE ELEMENT WHEN SHERRY AND

SHERRY-SOAKED CURRANTS ARE ADDED TO THE MIXTURE. AS THE PIE COOKS, THE CURRANTS SINK AND REST

ON THE BOTTOM. WHEN THE PIE IS SERVED, MORE ARE SPRINKLED ACROSS THE TOP.

1 unbaked 9-inch pastry shell

1/2 cup dried currants

1/4 cup dry sherry

1-3/4 cups homemade or canned pumpkin puree

1/2 cup granulated sugar

1/2 cup firmly packed brown sugar

1/2 teaspoon salt

1 teaspoon freshly ground cinnamon

1/2 teaspoon grated fresh ginger

1/2 teaspoon freshly grated nutmeg

2 eggs, lightly beaten

1 cup evaporated milk

1/4 cup water

Whipped cream for serving (optional)

Preheat the oven to 450°F. Put the currants in a small bowl and pour the sherry over them. Set aside.

In a large saucepan, cook the pumpkin puree over medium heat, stirring until it becomes dry and begins to caramelize slightly, about 10 minutes. Stirring constantly to prevent sticking and burning, add the sugars, salt, cinnamon, ginger, and nutmeg to the hot puree. Remove from heat. In a bowl, combine the eggs, milk, water, all of the sherry and half of the currants. Beat this mixture into the pan with the pumpkin mixture.

Pour the filling into a pastry-lined pie pan. Bake the pie for 15 minutes at 450°F. Reduce heat to 300°F and bake for about 45 minutes. Test the pie for doneness by gently shaking it to see how much of the center is still liquid. When only 1 inch still shakes, remove the pie; the center will finish cooking outside the oven.

Transfer the pie to a wire rack to cool for at least 20 minutes. Top with the remaining currants, and if desired, whipped cream. *Serves 6*

Old-Fashioned Pumpkin Pie

THIS IS A PURIST PUMPKIN PIE, CONTAINING ONLY PUMPKIN, SPICES, EGGS, AND MILK.
GRINDING THE SPICES YOURSELF BRINGS AN INCREDIBLE AROMA TO THE KITCHEN AND A CLEAN, FRESH FLAVOR
TO THE PIE. ONCE BAKED, IT CAN BE SERVED PLAIN OR WITH WHIPPED CREAM OR ICE CREAM AND
TOPPED WITH PECANS, WALNUTS, OR HAZELNUTS, IF YOU LIKE.

1 unbaked 9-inch pastry shell

1-3/4 cup homemade or canned
pumpkin puree

3/4 cup sugar

1/2 teaspoon salt

1 teaspoon freshly ground cinnamon

1/2 teaspoon freshly ground dried ginger

2 eggs

1 cup evaporated milk

1/2 cup water

Preheat an oven to 450°F. In a large saucepan, cook the pumpkin puree over medium heat for about 10 minutes, stirring until it becomes dry and begins to caramelize slightly. Stirring constantly to prevent sticking and burning, add the sugar, salt, cinnamon, and ginger to the hot puree. Remove from heat. In a medium bowl, beat together the eggs, milk, and water. Beat this into the pumpkin mixture.

Pour the filling into a pastry-lined pie pan. Bake the pie for 15 minutes. Reduce the oven temperature to 300°F and bake for about 45 minutes. Test the pie for doneness by gently shaking it to see how much of the center is still liquid. When only 1 inch still shakes, remove the pie; the center will finish cooking outside the oven. Let cool on a wire rack for at least 20 minutes before serving. *Serves 6*

Pumpkin Ice Cream

THIS ICE CREAM, RICH WITH PUMPKIN, SPICES, AND BROWN SUGAR,

IS A PERFECT DESSERT FOR A FALL OR WINTER DINNER.

2 cups heavy cream

2 cups milk

1-1/4 cups firmly packed brown sugar

1/4 teaspoon salt

4 egg yolks

2 cups homemade or canned
pumpkin puree

1/4 teaspoon ground mace

1 teaspoon grated nutmeg

1/4 teaspoon ground cloves

1/4 teaspoon ground ginger

Whipped cream for garnish

1/2 cup (2 ounces) chopped walnuts
or pecans (optional)

In a large, heavy-bottomed saucepan, combine the cream, milk, brown sugar, and salt. Bring to a boil over medium-high heat, stirring often, until the brown sugar has dissolved. In a small bowl, whisk the egg yolks together until they pale in color. Gradually whisk about 1 cup of the hot milk mixture into the yolks. Now, whisk the hot yolk mixture into the hot milk mixture, and cook, stirring constantly, until the mixture coats the back of a spoon. Remove from heat and let cool to lukewarm.

Put the pumpkin puree in a medium bowl and whisk in 1 cup of the milk mixture. Whisk the pumpkin mixture and the spices into the milk mixture. Freeze in an ice cream maker according to the manufacturer's instructions.

To serve, scoop the ice cream into bowls and top with whipped cream, and if desired, a sprinkling of walnuts. *Makes 8 servings*

pumpkins for kids

7

Painted and Appliquéd Pumpkins

THIS SIMPLE, FUN WAY TO DECORATE PUMPKINS IS A GREAT ACTIVITY FOR HALLOWEEN PARTIES, AS CHILDREN CAN TAKE THEIR PUMPKINS HOME AS PARTY FAVORS.

YOU WILL NEED:

Pumpkins

Acrylic paints and permanent markers

Paintbrushes and a dish of water

Scissors

Craft glue

Glitter

Fake fur

Pipe cleaners

Shaky craft eyes

Buttons, rickrack, and other sewing notions

TO MAKE:

Give the children a number of pumpkins and a box of the above craft supplies and let them create.

Halloween Cookie Tree

IT'S HARD TO TELL WHICH CHILDREN ENJOY MORE, MAKING AND DECORATING THE COOKIES OR CREATING A "MONSTER" TREE, THEN EATING THE COOKIES! THIS TREE ALSO MAKES A FESTIVE HOLIDAY CENTERPIECE TO GREET AND FEED VISITING TRICK-OR-TREATERS.

YOU WILL NEED:

Floral foam blocks

Old metal pail or bucket

Several gnarled old branches

Spanish or lichen moss

20-gauge florist wire, cut into 5-inch lengths

Candles (menorah or small tapers)

Candle-sticking wax

Halloween cookies (page 101) made
   with a hole in the top for threading

Cord or narrow ribbon

TO MAKE:

Cut the floral blocks to fit the pail or bucket and fill pail almost to the top with the blocks.

Stick the branches into the dry floral blocks and insert them deep enough so that they are held securely in place. Fill the top of the bucket around the base of the branches with enough moss to cover the blocks.

Wrap pieces of wire tightly onto the branches at different levels, then form each piece of wire into an upright coil to hold a candle in place. Make sure there are no pieces of branch above the candleholders. Insert the candles into the wire coils and affix them with the candle-sticking wax.

Thread the cookies with cord or ribbon and hang at different places on the branches. Light the candles.

Papier-Mâché Trick-or-Treat Baskets

THIS IS A GREAT TWO-PART ACTIVITY TO
DO WITH CHILDREN OF ALL AGES.

YOU WILL NEED:

Large balloons

Petroleum jelly

Newspaper (cut into 6-inch strips,
1 inch and 1/2 inch wide)

Large bowl of water for newspaper strips

Small bowl for papier-mâché

Flour

Acrylic paints and brushes

Scissors

Ice pick or paper-hole punch

Twisted green crepe paper, including one
piece about 40 inches long for the handle

Adhesive tape

Green pipe cleaners

TO MAKE:

STEP 1 Blow up a balloon and cover it
with a thin layer of petroleum jelly. Soak
the newspaper in the bowl of water. In
the small bowl, mix water and flour into a
paste that has the consistency of batter.

Dip wet newspaper strips into the
paste and lay them around the bottom
two-thirds of the balloon. This may take
6 to 8 layers of strips. Let dry completely.
A hair dryer can be used to speed drying.

STEP 2 Paint the basket. Pop the balloon after the paint dries.

STEP 3 Cut a decorative edge around
the top of the basket. With the ice pick
or paper-hole punch, make 2 holes at
least 1 inch from the upper edge and on
opposite sides of the basket. Insert the
crepe paper for the handle into one hole,
then pull it to its midpoint. Twist strands
around each other to form braided
handle, and knot ends through other
hole on inside of basket.

STEP 4 Make leaves by untwisting 6-
inch lengths of crepe paper and cutting
them into leaf shapes with short stems.
Attach leaves to handle with tape. Form
vine tendrils by winding pipe cleaners
around your finger. Attach tendril ends to
handle near leaves.

breads, muffins, & cookies

Pumpkin and Pecan Pancakes

LIGHT AND FLUFFY, THESE PALE ORANGE PANCAKES ARE WELL SEASONED WITH NUTMEG AND CLOVES.

FOR THE BEST FLAVOR, GRIND THE SPICES YOURSELF.

1/4 cup chopped pecans

1 cup all-purpose flour

2-1/2 teaspoons baking powder

1/2 teaspoon salt

1-1/2 tablespoons sugar

1/2 teaspoon grated nutmeg

1/2 teaspoon ground cloves

1 egg

1 cup milk

1/2 cup homemade or canned pumpkin puree

3 tablespoons canola or other light vegetable oil

Vegetable oil for cooking

Butter and syrup (maple, boysenberry, or blackberry) for serving

In a small, dry skillet over medium heat, toast the pecans, stirring often, until slightly browned, 3 or 4 minutes. Remove from the heat and set aside.

Sift the flour, baking powder, salt, sugar, nutmeg, and cloves together into a small bowl. In another bowl, beat the egg, milk, and pumpkin together until just blended. Stir in the oil. Add the flour mixture all at once to the egg mixture and stir until just blended.

Heat a griddle or a large skillet over medium-high heat. Coat with vegetable oil. Drop a small bit of pancake batter onto the griddle or skillet. If it sizzles and puffs, remove it and add the pancake batter 1/4 cup at a time. Cook until the edges pull slightly away from the pan and bubbles form evenly on the top, 1 or 2 minutes. Turn and cook on the second side until golden brown. Transfer to a serving platter and keep warm. Repeat until all the batter is used.

Serve at once accompanied by butter, syrup, and toasted pecans. *Makes about 1 dozen pancakes*

Halloween Cookies

TASTY BUTTER COOKIES CUT INTO PUMPKINS AND
OTHER HALLOWEEN SHAPES MAKE FESTIVE TREATS FOR TRICK-OR-TREATERS OR
GHOULISH ORNAMENTS FOR A HALLOWEEN COOKIE TREE.

1-3/4 cups sifted all-purpose flour

1/2 teaspoon baking powder

1/4 teaspoon salt

2/3 cups butter at room temperature

1/2 cup granulated sugar

1 egg

FROSTING

2 cups confectioners' sugar, sifted

4 tablespoons milk, plus more
as needed

food coloring as desired

Preheat an oven to 400°F. Sift the flour with the baking powder and salt together onto a piece of wax paper. In a medium bowl, cream the butter and granulated sugar together until light and fluffy. Beat in the egg, then add the flour mixture in thirds, each time stirring until the dough is smooth.

On a lightly floured board, roll the dough to a thickness of 1/8 inch. Cut into desired cookie shapes and put them on an ungreased baking sheet. If you are making cookies to hang on a cookie tree, use an ice pick to make a 1/4-inch diameter hole in each one. Gather up the scraps of dough and roll them out again until all the dough is used.

Bake just until lightly browned on the bottom and pale golden on top, 6 to 8 minutes. Let the cookies cool on the pan for 5 minutes, then transfer them to wire racks.

To make the frosting, put the confectioners' sugar in a medium bowl and stir in milk until a stiff but spreadable paste forms. Though it may seem overly stiff, too much milk will make an unworkable frosting. If more milk is necessary, add only 1/2 teaspoon at a time. Divide the frosting among separate bowls and color as desired. To make an almost black frosting, use equal amounts of red and green food coloring. Frost either warm or cooled cookies. If the cookies are warm, the frosting will spread more easily. *Makes about 36 cookies*

Pumpkin Bars with Lemon Glaze

A SWEET-TART LEMON GLAZE ADDS A COMPLEMENTARY FLAVOR

TO THESE MOIST FRUIT-AND-NUT-FILLED BARS.

1 egg

1 cup sugar

1 cup canola or other light vegetable oil

1-1/3 cups (8 ounces) pitted dates,
finely chopped

1-3/4 cups all-purpose flour

1 teaspoon baking soda

1 teaspoon salt

1 teaspoon ground cinnamon

1 teaspoon ground cloves

1 cup homemade or
canned pumpkin puree

1 cup (4 ounces) chopped walnuts

1 cup confectioners' sugar, sifted,
plus more as needed

2 tablespoons fresh lemon juice

Preheat the oven to 350°F. Grease a 10-inch-by-15-inch jelly roll pan. In a large bowl, beat the egg. Stir in the sugar, oil, and dates. In a medium bowl, stir together the flour, baking soda, and spices. Add the egg mixture and the pumpkin puree alternately to the flour mixture in thirds, stirring to blend well each time. Stir in the nuts.

Pour the batter into the prepared pan and spread it evenly with a spatula. Bake until well browned and a toothpick inserted in the center comes out clean, about 25 minutes. Transfer the pan to a rack to cool for about 5 minutes.

To make the glaze, in a small bowl, mix the confectioners' sugar and lemon juice. If the glaze seems too thin, add a little more sugar. Spread the glaze over the baked layer.

Let stand for 5 minutes, then cut into bars about 3 inches by 1-1/2 inches. *Makes about 30 bars*

Pumpkin and Medjool Date Muffins

INTENSELY SWEET DATES STUD THESE PUMPKIN-SPICE MUFFINS, A GOOD BREAKFAST OR TEATIME TREAT.

IF DESIRED, SPREAD THE MUFFINS WITH A FAVORITE FROSTING TO SERVE AS A DESSERT.

1-1/2 cups all-purpose flour

1/2 cup granulated sugar

2 teaspoons baking powder

1/2 teaspoon salt

1 teaspoon ground allspice

3/4 cup chopped, pitted Medjool dates

1/2 cup (2 ounces) chopped pecans

1/2 cup milk

4 tablespoons butter, melted and cooled

2 tablespoons grated orange zest

1 egg

1/2 cup homemade or canned pumpkin puree

1-1/2 teaspoons orange juice

Preheat the oven to 325°F. Liberally butter 12 standard muffin cups with butter or line them with paper liners. Sift the flour, sugar, baking powder, salt, and allspice together into a large bowl. Add the dates and pecans and stir them in until coated with flour. In a smaller bowl, stir the milk, melted butter, orange zest, egg, pumpkin puree, and orange juice until well mixed.

Add the wet ingredients to the flour mixture and stir with a fork just until the dry ingredients are moistened. The batter should be slightly lumpy. Spoon the batter into the prepared muffin cups, filling them two-thirds full.

Bake until well browned and a toothpick inserted into the middle of a muffin comes out clean, 15 to 18 minutes. Let cool in the pan on a rack or counter. Serve warm or at room temperature. *Makes 12 muffins*

Pumpkin Bread

THIS RICH, MOIST BREAD, WELL-SPICED AND DOTTED WITH PLUMP RAISINS, IS BAKED IN A BUNDT PAN, THEN DUSTED WITH

CONFECTIONERS' SUGAR. IF POSSIBLE, GRIND THE SPICES YOURSELF IN A SPICE GRINDER OR COFFEE GRINDER

RESERVED FOR THAT PURPOSE. SERVE SLICES TOPPED WITH PIECES OF CHEDDAR CHEESE, SPREAD WITH CREAM CHEESE,

OR SIMPLY PLAIN. FOR DESSERT, SERVE IT WITH ICE CREAM OR POACHED FRUIT SUCH AS APPLES OR PEARS.

1/2 cup (1 stick) plus 1 tablespoon butter
at room temperature

2 cups firmly packed brown sugar

2 eggs

1 teaspoon vanilla extract

1-1/2 cups grated apple (about 2 apples)

1-inch piece fresh ginger, peeled and grated

1-1/2 teaspoons fresh lemon juice

1-1/2 cups homemade or canned
pumpkin puree

2 cups all-purpose flour

1/2 teaspoon salt

1 teaspoon baking soda

1/2 teaspoon ground cinnamon

1/2 teaspoon ground cloves

1/2 teaspoon grated nutmeg

2 teaspoons grated lemon zest

3/4 cup raisins

Confectioners' sugar for dusting

Preheat the oven to 350°F. In a large bowl, cream the butter with a wooden spoon. Add the brown sugar, eggs, vanilla, apples, ginger, lemon juice, and pumpkin puree, stirring to blend well. (Alternatively, in the same order, process the ingredients in a food processor just long enough to blend them well, then transfer the mixture to a large bowl.) Sift together the flour, salt, baking soda, cinnamon, cloves, and nutmeg directly onto the wet ingredients, then stir until thoroughly blended. Stir in the lemon zest and raisins. Pour into a 9-inch bundt pan.

Bake until the cake is puffed and brown, the surface springs back when pushed gently with the tip of your finger, and the cake is just slightly pulling away from the edges of the pan, about 1 hour. Let the cake cool in the pan on a rack for 10 minutes. Invert the pan onto the rack to unmold the cake; if necessary, first slide a thin-bladed knife around the edge of the pan to loosen the cake sides. Place the cake upright on the rack to cool.

To serve, transfer to a serving plate and dust the top with confectioners' sugar. *Serves 20 to 24*

Metric Conversion Table

LIQUID WEIGHTS

U.S. Measurements	Metric Equivalents
1/4 teaspoon	1.23 ml
1/2 teaspoon	2.5 ml
3/4 teaspoon	3.7 ml
1 teaspoon	5 ml
1 dessertspoon	10 ml
1 tablespoon (3 teaspoons)	15 ml
2 tablespoons (1 ounce)	30 ml
1/4 cup	60 ml
1/3 cup	80 ml
1/2 cup	120 ml
2/3 cup	160 ml
3/4 cup	180 ml
1 cup (8 ounces)	240 ml
2 cups (1 pint)	480 ml
3 cups	720 ml
4 cups (1 quart)	1 liter
4 quarts (1 gallon)	33/4 liters

DRY WEIGHTS

U.S. Measurements	Metric Equivalents
1/4 ounce	7 grams
1/3 ounce	10 grams
1/2 ounce	14 grams
1 ounce	28 grams
1-1/2 ounces	42 grams
1-3/4 ounces	50 grams
2 ounces	57 grams
3-1/2 ounces	100 grams
4 ounces (1/4 pound)	114 grams
6 ounces	170 grams
8 ounces (1/2 pound)	227 grams
9 ounces	250 grams
16 ounces (1 pound)	464 grams

TEMPERATURES

Fahrenheit	Celsius (Centigrade)
32°F (water freezes)	0°C
200°F	95°C
212°F (water boils)	100°C
250°F	120°C
275°F	135°C
300°F (slow oven)	150°C
325°F	160°C
350°F (moderate oven)	175°C
375°F	190°C
400°F (hot oven)	205°C
425°F	220°C
450°F (very hot oven)	230°C
475°F	245°C
500°F (extremely hot oven)	260°C

LENGTH

U.S. Measurements	Metric Equivalents
1/8 inch	3 mm
1/4 inch	6 mm
3/8 inch	1 cm
1/2 inch	1.2 cm
3/4 inch	2 cm
1 inch	2.5 cm
1-1/4 inches	3.1 cm
1-1/2 inches	3.7 cm
2 inches	5 cm
3 inches	7.5 cm
4 inches	10 cm

APPROXIMATE EQUIVALENTS

1 kilo is slightly more than 2 pounds.

1 liter is slightly more than 1 quart.

1 centimeter is approximately 3/8 inch.

List of Recipes

Soups and Stews

Beef and Pumpkin Stew with
   Pomegranates, 21–22
Pumpkin and Black Bean Soup, 18
Pumpkin-Ginger Soup Topped with Crème
   Fraîche and Condiments, 16
Pumpkin Soup Topped with Croutons and
   Fresh Thyme, 19
Roasted Pumpkin Seeds, 23
Root Vegetable and Pumpkin Ragout,
   28–29

Salads

Butterhead Lettuce and Pumpkin
   Blossom Salad, 26
Frisée Salad with Deep-Fried Pumpkin
   Bits and Lardons, 25
Spinach and Pumpkin Seed Salad, 24

First Courses

Baked Pumpkins Stuffed with Sausage
   and Sage, 59
Pumpkin and Chanterelle Mushroom
   Risotto, 49
Pumpkin Blossoms with Goat Cheese
   Filling, 56

Side Dishes

Baked Pumpkins Stuffed with Sausage
   and Sage, 59
Honey-Grilled Pumpkin Slices, 46
Pumpkin and Chanterelle Mushroom
   Risotto, 49
Pumpkin and Mixed Winter Squash Filled
   with Savory Puree, 55
Scalloped Pumpkin and Potatoes, 52
Whipped Pumpkin on Caramelized
   Onions with Spicy Walnuts, 57

Main Courses

Baked Pumpkins Stuffed with Sausage
   and Sage, 59
Grilled Quail with Herbed Mashed
   Pumpkin, 60
Pumpkin and Chanterelle Mushroom
   Risotto, 49
Pumpkin Pasta with Baby Bok Choy,
   Prosciutto, and Pecans, 51
Sautéed Pumpkin, Red Peppers, and
   Greens with Polenta, 48

Desserts

Harvest Pie, 83
Old-Fashioned Pumpkin Pie, 85
Pumpkin Cheesecake in a Gingersnap-
   Walnut Crust, 78
Pumpkin-Filled Phyllo Cups, 81
Pumpkin Flan, 82
Pumpkin Ice Cream, 86

Cookies

Halloween Cookies, 101
Pumpkin Bars with Lemon Glaze, 102

Breads and Muffins

Pumpkin and Medjool Date Muffins, 105
Pumpkin and Pecan Pancakes, 98
Pumpkin Bread, 106

List of Crafts

Tabletop Pumpkins

Pumpkin Candle Holders, 35
Pumpkin Place Cards, 32
Pumpkin Soup Tureen with Mini-Pumpkin
   Condiment Bowls, 36
Pumpkin Vase, 43
Three Pumpkin Centerpieces, 39–40

Outdoor Pumpkins

Hanging Mini Monsters, 69
Parchment- or Tissue-Lined
   Jack-O'-Lanterns, 70
Pumpkin Harvest Swag, 67
Pumpkin Wreath, 64
Wood-Carving Jack-O'-Lanterns, 73

Pumpkins for Kids

Halloween Cookie Tree, 93
Painted and Appliquéd Pumpkins, 90
Papier-Mâché Trick-or-Treat Baskets, 94

Index

All Hallows' Eve, 9

Baby bok choy
  Pumpkin Pasta with Baby Bok Choy,
    Prosciutto, and Pecans, 51
Baking pumpkins, 11
Baskets
  Papier-Mâché Trick-or-Treat Baskets,
    92–93
Baum, Frank L., 9
Beans
  Pumpkin and Black Bean Soup, 18
Beef
  Beef and Pumpkin Stew with
    Pomegranates, 21–22
Big Max pumpkin, 10
Boston Pie pumpkin, 10
Bowls
  Pumpkin Soup Tureen with Mini-Pumpkin
    Condiment Bowls, 36
Bread
  Pumpkin Bread, 106
Butterhead lettuce
  Butterhead Lettuce and Pumpkin
    Blossom Salad, 26
Buying pumpkins, 10

Candle holders
  Pumpkin Candle Holders, 35
Centerpieces
  Three pumpkin centerpieces, 39–40
Chanterelle mushrooms
  Pumpkin and Chanterelle Mushroom
    Risotto, 49
Cheese pumpkins, 10
Cheese-box pumpkins, 10
Cheesecake
  Pumpkin Cheesecake in a Gingersnap-
    Walnut Crust, 78
Cinderella, 9, 10
Cookie tree
  Halloween Cookie Tree, 93

Cookies
  Halloween Cookies, 101
  Pumpkin Bars with Lemon Glaze, 102
Cooking-pumpkin varieties, 10
Cooking with pumpkin blossoms, 12
Cooking with pumpkins, 10, 11
Crane, Ichabod, 9
Crème fraîche
  Pumpkin-Ginger Soup Topped with Crème
    Fraîche and Condiments, 16
Croutons
  Pumpkin Soup Topped with Croutons and
    Fresh Thyme, 19

Dates
  Pumpkin and Medjool Date Muffins, 105
Decorated pumpkins
  Painted and Appliquéd Pumpkins, 90
Desserts
  Harvest Pie, 83
  Old-Fashioned Pumpkin Pie, 85
  Pumpkin Cheesecake in a Gingersnap-
    Walnut Crust, 78
  Pumpkin-Filled Phyllo Cups, 81
  Pumpkin Flan, 82
  Pumpkin Ice Cream, 86

Flan
  Pumpkin Flan, 82
Frisée
  Frisée Salad with Deep-Fried Pumpkin Bits
    and Lardons, 25

Ginger
  Pumpkin-Ginger Soup Topped with Crème
    Fraîche and Condiments, 16
Gingersnaps
  Pumpkin Cheesecake in a Gingersnap-
    Walnut Crust, 78
Goat cheese
  Pumpkin Blossoms with Goat Cheese
    Filling, 56

Greens
  Sautéed Pumpkin, Red Peppers, and
    Greens with Polenta, 48

Halloween, 9
  Halloween Cookies, 101
  Halloween Cookie Tree, 93
Honey
  Honey-Grilled Pumpkin Slices, 46

Ice cream
  Pumpkin Ice Cream, 86
Irving, Washington, 9

Jack-Be-Little pumpkin, 10
Jack-O'-Lantern pumpkin, 9
Jack-o'-lanterns, 9
  Hanging Mini-Monsters, 69
  Parchment- or Tissue-Lined
    Jack-O'-Lanterns, 70
  Wood-Carving Jack-O'-Lanterns, 73

Lardons
  Frisée Salad with Deep-Fried Pumpkin Bits
    and Lardons, 25

Monsters
  Hanging Mini Monsters, 69
Muffins
  Pumpkin and Medjool Date Muffins, 105
Muscade pumpkin, 10
Musqué de Provence pumpkin, 10

New England Pie pumpkin, 10
Northeast Pie pumpkin, 10
Nuts
  Pumpkin and Pecan Pancakes, 98
  Pumpkin Cheesecake in a Gingersnap-
    Walnut Crust, 78
  Pumpkin Pasta with Baby Bok Choy,
    Prosciutto, and Pecans, 51
  Spicy Walnuts, 57

Onions
    Whipped Pumpkin on Caramelized Onions
        with Spicy Walnuts, 57

Painted pumpkins
    Painted and Appliquéd Pumpkins, 90
Pancakes
    Pumpkin and Pecan Pancakes, 98
Papier-mâché
    Papier-Mâché Trick-or-Treat Baskets, 94
Parchment paper
    Parchment- or Tissue-Lined
        Jack-O'-Lanterns, 70
Pasta
    Pumpkin Pasta with Baby Bok Choy,
        Prosciutto, and Pecans, 51
Phyllo
    Pumpkin-Filled Phyllo Cups, 81
Pie pumpkins, 10
Pies
    Harvest Pie, 83
    Old-Fashioned Pumpkin Pie, 85
Pilgrims, 9, 10
Place cards
    Pumpkin Place Cards, 32
Polenta
    Sautéed Pumpkin, Red Peppers, and
        Greens with Polenta, 48
Pomegranates
    Beef and Pumpkin Stew with
        Pomegranates, 21–22
Potatoes
    Scalloped Pumpkin and Potatoes, 52
Prosciutto
    Pumpkin Pasta with Baby Bok Choy,
        Prosciutto, and Pecans, 51
Pumpkin blossoms, 12
    Butterhead Lettuce and Pumpkin
        Blossom Salad, 26
    Pumpkin Blossoms with Goat Cheese
        Filling, 56
Pumpkinhead, Jack, 9

Pumpkin puree, preparing and storing, 11
Pumpkin seeds
    Roasted Pumpkin Seeds, 23
    Spinach and Pumpkin Seed Salad, 24
Pumpkin varieties, 9, 10

Quail
    Grilled Quail with Herbed Mashed
        Pumpkin, 60

Ragout
    Root Vegetable and Pumpkin Ragout,
        28–29
Raw pumpkin, preparing, 12
Red peppers
    Sautéed Pumpkin, Red Peppers, and
        Greens with Polenta, 48
Risotto
    Pumpkin and Chanterelle Mushroom
        Risotto, 49
Root vegetables; see also onions, potatoes
    Root Vegetable and Pumpkin Ragout,
        28–29
Rouge Vif d'Etampes pumpkin, 10

Sage
    Baked Pumpkins Stuffed with Sausage
        and Sage, 59
Salads
    Butterhead Lettuce and Pumpkin
        Blossom Salad, 26
    Frisée Salad with Deep-Fried Pumpkin Bits
        and Lardons, 25
    Spinach and Pumpkin Seed Salad, 24
Sausage
    Baked Pumpkins Stuffed with Sausage
        and Sage, 59
Small Sugar pumpkin, 10

Soup
    Pumpkin and Black Bean Soup, 18
    Pumpkin-Ginger Soup Topped with Crème
        Fraîche and Condiments, 16
    Pumpkin Soup Topped with Croutons and
        Fresh Thyme, 19
Steaming pumpkin, 12
Stew
    Beef and Pumpkin Stew with
        Pomegranates, 21–22
    Root Vegetable and Pumpkin Ragout,
        28–29
Storing pumpkins, 11
Squash blossoms, see pumpkin blossoms
Sugar Pie pumpkin, 10
Sugar pumpkins, 10
Swag
    Pumpkin Harvest Swag, 67

Thyme
    Pumpkin Soup Topped with Croutons and
        Fresh Thyme, 19
Trick-or-Treat Baskets
    Papier-Mâché Trick-or-Treat Baskets, 94
Tureen
    Pumpkin Soup Tureen with Mini-Pumpkin
        Condiment Bowls, 36

Vase
    Pumpkin Vase, 43

Winter squash, 10
    Pumpkin and Mixed Winter Squash Filled
        with Savory Puree, 55
Wreath
    Pumpkin Wreath, 64